# MUSINGS OF A WAYFARER

BUSHRA. A

Copyright © Bushra. A
All Rights Reserved.

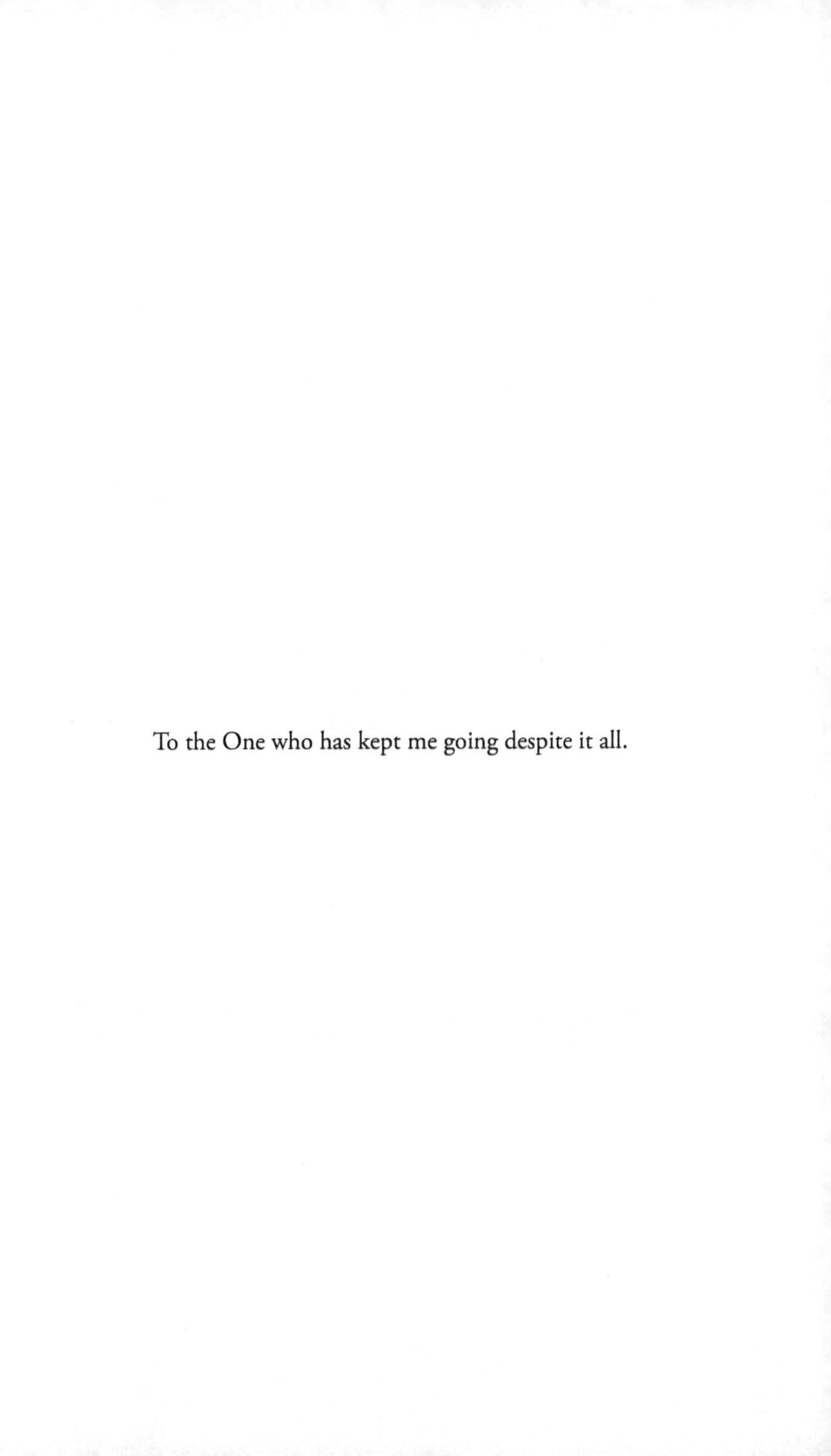

To the One who has kept me going despite it all.

# Contents

# Contents

# Contents

# Contents

# 1. Art

She was art,
art he could paint
all day long;
sophistication
he'd love to face.
Such intricate designs,
vibrant colours,
love that could leave
anyone dazed.

*It was a pity*
*he was colour blind.*

# 2. Untold And Unseen

• 2 •

My tutor or my friend?
My parent or my companion?
I'm at loss for words
For you seem to be all of them.

My unseen teacher,
My mentor, my guide;
Solving unspoken problems,
Always by my side.

Ever shouldering
And an ever solutioning friend;
Always there for me,
Always on the blend.

Extremely caring
And nurturing when I fall;
When evaded by loneliness,
You seem to shift it all.

There for me twenty four seven,
Three sixty five days in a year;
Even when others have no time for me,

You know of my every tear.

Instilling confidence in me,
Sculpting my life,　　　　　• 3 •
Controlling my behaviour
And people's entry, exit in my life.

More than a tutor, more than a friend,
More than a parent or a companion;
I still can't find the right word, Ya Rabb,
For you're all of them in unison.

# 3. Blurred Words



Dark minds
Constricted hearts
Racing horses
Poisoned tarts.

Fluttering heartbeats
Deceiving eyes
Useless expectations
Betraying ties.

Loud mouths
Narrowed gaze
Unending gossips
Never-ending chase.

Infinite people
Heavy hearts
Endless endings
Handful starts.

Empty promises
Meaningless hopes
Blinding light

Binding ropes.

Pointless musings
Bookish dreams
Dirty scars
Silent screams.

Pinched expressions
Pained smiles
Untrue illusions
Unending miles.

Soiled thoughts
Unclear gaze
Cruel intentions
Mirrored maze.

Numerous humans
Sinking faith
Blurred images
Haunting wraith.

Sobbing mess
Salty trails
Dried ducts —
All unheard tales.

# 4. Gratitude Or Grief?

• 6 •

There are days when I feel
Like the most blessed person on earth,
And then there are days when all I want to do
Is curl into a ball and cry.

But then again, I think of all those
Who've been approached by their death unsuspectingly
And I couldn't help but feel grateful to Him
For letting me see another day go by.

# 5. Iceberg

The world — it only knew a part of her:
The tip of the iceberg that was shown,
But in truth, forget the ocean that hid the giant mass,
She was an entire galaxy on her own.

# 6. Wishful Thinking

Most days
I have this insane sort of
Desire in me
To vanish into thin air,
Poof!
And be gone
Without a trace;
Just like that,
Leaving no clue.
At least then,
I do hope
The things that haunt me
Cease to exist;
If not in this world,
Then at least
In the eyes of my
Hopeful,
Wishful,
Observing self.

# 7. Cages

Our hearts
are such
vicious, manipulative creatures.
Maybe that was why
He created them
inside cages.

# 8. Cacophony

If you cannot see through
The smiles I fake,
The pain I mask,
The facade I put up —
You do not deserve my love.

If you cannot sense
The agony I go through,
The fire I burn in,
My charred remains —
You do not deserve my care.

If you cannot feel
The numerous times
I pretend as if
Everything is alright —
You do not deserve my trust.

If you cannot hear
My silent screams,
My thudding heart,
The mute whimpers
That escape me —

You do not deserve my hope.

If you do not know
The way I barely manage
To keep going ignoring my pain,
Trying to keep myself
From falling, from breaking down —
You most definitely
Do not deserve me in your life.

*Maybe I should stop*
*Expecting*
*After all this time.*

# 9. Confuzzled

It gets too intense —
Myriad of emotions
Swirling, unsettling
When the heart speaks a language
The mind cannot decipher.

# 10. Amends

I have reached a phase
I care no more.
Surprisingly, it's so comforting.
I have reached a phase,
It hurts no more.
I never expected it to be so soothing.
My rage has passed,
It burns no more.
I never expected such an ending.
My longing is gone,
It stings no more
Though the bond we shared was quite touching.
My love has expired,
I think of you no more.
When it stayed, it stayed heartrending.
When you had barged into my life,
I was not able to think anymore
But now, I'm gradually changing!

I'm resurrecting the walls around my heart,
I'm letting my mind reign once again.
Discarding the hopes I had started to collect,
I'm treading on in life's path again.

I had never wanted to expect from life —
That was one rule I have failed to abide,
For I was convinced
That even the greatest human to exist
Had someone like you by his side.
In reality, I was quite taken by the idea of 'you'
That I had actually failed to see:
You were only an illusion,
We were never meant to be.

# 11. Revival

I keep falling
into a deep abyss,
subdued by the world
without any control
but you revive me, Oh Lord,
every single time!
My faith serves
as binding chords
pulling me back on to track,
healing my torn parts,
helping me through darkness.
Indeed, Oh Lord,
You are the most Sublime.

# 12. Deal

If you've gained everything
But lost God,
What have you gained at all?

# 13. The Maker's Plan



If you are granted what you were praying for,

Be grateful to Allaah.

It was what was good for you.

And if you aren't granted what you were praying for,

Be especially grateful to Allaah.

It was what was best for you.


*You never know what He was protecting you from.*

# 14. Ignorance

I break down in front of my Lord
When I pray.
I whimper
Into the dead of the night.
I toss and turn around
In restlessness and anxiety,
Contemplating things
You never get right.

There are hundreds of paths
I'd rather not tread,
There are hundreds of things
I'd rather not say.
There are hundreds of tears
I'd rather not shed,
But this is something
I'm clueless as to how to convey.

I'm scared of the things
That you could bring into my life.
I'm scared of my dreams
That you might scatter.
It's clear that your dreams don't match mine,

Not one bit; no.
It is okay, let me be,
Don't let me shatter.


You have no idea of the grip
This invisible noose has on me.
I'm not even certain
If you are not aware of it
Or pretend not to see.
Whatever it is, don't let me go,
I need time to gather my pieces.
I don't ask for anything else,
Please let me be.

# 15. Irrevocable

Sometimes
People think so much
Of this temporary life,
Pile up too many
Unrealistic expectations,
Weave so many dreams
That depict fairy tales
And when reality
Finally dawns upon them,
As it was always meant to be,
It leaves them
Irrevocably shattered.
And they are left
Longing, yearning
But never once belonging
To the life they once thought
Could be theirs.

# 16. Misted Days

Some days
I think of giving up
Simply because
The pressure makes it too difficult
To breathe.
Most days
I thirst
To live life
My own way
Not letting anyone rule over me.
But almost every other day
I stand and watch from afar
People trampling all over me,
Leaving me with scars to last a lifetime
And on these days,
Even irony has a laugh at me.

# 17. I Will Go On

• 22 •

The world burdens me —
I get choked and suffocated.
It's difficult to breathe and to see
But I have to go on.

Each day my going gets tough,
I dissolve into oblivion;
My paths diverge, get rough
But I will have to go on.

Charred hopes and broken dreams,
Are all what remains of me now
Or so it seems.
I have to gather myself and go on.

I refuse to be a cast-off,
I get shattered when I'm one;
Disguising my trembling voice,
I make an effort to go on.

Even though I'm nobody to most,
The Almighty keeps watch;
I'm alone with no sign of the coast.

Braving all odds, I have to go on.


Agony, angst, fear and trepidation —
I could barely brace myself now
From all these simmering emotions
But I choose to go on.


I'm in possesssion of a fragile heart,
I hate being shown false hope
And then being torn apart.
Putting it all in the past, I will move on.


There is always light at the end of a tunnel,
The dreary nights do come to an end.
My silver linings will arrive for sure, that much I could tell.
Believing in it, I will go on.

# 18. The Writer

There is peace in knowing
That He was the One
Who wrote all our stories.

# 19. Truly?

You appear to me as a dream,
I'm scared to open my eyes
And find you gone.

# 20. Change

My Lord knows
I have no idea
How
You went from being
A spark of hope in my heart
To
A constant prayer on my lips,
My Lord knows.

# 21. Adulting

How foolish
Had I been
To believe that
My problems would exist
Only until I grow up.

No one ever told me
Of the monsters
I'd have to face,
Of the comfort
I'd have to sacrifice,
Or even of my dreams
That I'd have to set aside.

How foolish
Had I been
To believe that
My problems would exist
Only until I grow up.

# 22. Assurance



There is so much of
Intense pain
In my being;
My heart threatens to
Burst from its seems.
Had not the assurance
Come from my Lord
That the world is naught
But a prison
For the believers,
I know not
Where I would have been.

# 23. Broken Promises

• 29 •

Often times
it is not even about
the words that were thrown
or the hurt that was caused;
it's about
the promises that were broken
and the hopes that were lost.

# 24. Contentment

I take a moment
to think
of all the things
He has given me.
Suddenly,
my heart
feels too full
and my pocket —
heavy.

# 25. Don't Tell Me

Don't tell me you know me,
You have no idea who I am.
Don't tell me you get me,
There's a lot more you don't understand.
Don't tell me you trust me,
Your actions prove otherwise.
Don't tell me you believe me,
I can easily see through your lies.

Don't try to appease me,
There's nothing you can do.
Don't tell me it will pass,
I know that more than you.
Don't tell you feel me,
You know nothing of the scars I conceal.
Don't tell me you understand,
You know nothing of what I feel.

I drown in sorrow,
Feel the pain;
Get involved and,
Forget to refrain.
I know it's my fault,

But what can I do?
I can't adopt the tactics of the world,
I'm lost unlike you.

# 26. Footing

Do not hold
any malice,
or grudge
in your heart.
No matter what
the issue may be,
no one is worth
the strain
between you
and your Lord.

# 27. Nowhere Else

When I stand before my Lord,
Head bent, arms folded, gaze lowered,
I cannot think of being anywhere else,
Doing anything else.
He alone is capable of understanding me
Without the use of words
And I revel in it.
He alone loves me despite all my flaws.
It is what it is.

I commit mistakes, I sin and I repent;
I keep fighting off my demons on a regular basis
But at the end of the day
With everything said and done,
I find that
No one else understands me
More than Him.

He is always there
Looking out for me,
Helping me,
Shaping me,
Correcting me,

And never judging me;
Loving me for I truly am.


The One true Lord,
The Creator of the heavens and the earth;
The Controller of all my affairs.
He is there,
Just there for me
When no one truly is.

# 28. Mirage

The older you get,
the more
the picture
of this fake world
gets apparent.

# 29. Of Both Worlds

• 37 •

If He can take care
of all the worlds
and still think of you,
why can't you take care of your world alone
and think of Him too?

# 30. Never Them

In a span of two decades and more
I've spent on planet earth,
I have met countless of people
who've have served their purpose in my life —
from some, I learnt about
the goodness of the world,
from some, I have widened my knowledge,
few have urged me
to become a better version of myself
without knowing it themselves
and then, there are some
who have been highlighted on my list —
the ones I have sworn
to never become.

# 31. Masks

• 39 •

Maybe deep down
all we ever wanted
was their masks
to never fall off
their faces.

# 32. Rain Of Hope

They say when it rains,
It pours
And I find that
I cannot agree more.
Of course, it doesn't rain,
It pours;
With thunders and bolts.
Violent storms seem immminent,
The wind rages and howls.
Strongest of the strongest get uprooted
And you're left with situations
Unsuited.
But guess what?
If you don't take a stand for yourself,
No one's going to do it for you.
If you don't open your umbrella
And hold it over your head,
No one's going to do it for you.
If you don't voice your opinion
And stand up for your rights,
No one's going to do it for you.

Nothing would ever change

When you choose to sit back and moan.

If anything, you'd only be left feeling forlorn.

Make it a point to get up,

Do something about it.

Don't let it matter if people speak,

For at the end of the day,

It isn't their approval you seek.


*Remember Allaah only helps those who help themselves.*

# 33. Fruitless Expectations

I had expected the seasons to change,
the days to roll,
the calendars that we've hung on our walls
to be replaced by another,
one after the other.
I had expected the time to speed,
the world to change,
and if I were honest with myself,
even the Signs of the Hour to appear over the horizon.

I had expected a tight schedule,
multiplied responsiblities,
stuff that would prove too hard to juggle.
I had anticipated a rocky road,
several evasive turns,
a broken heart that would have seen
one too many a mending.

I had even expected for us to be waylaid by life,
to be robbed of our peace,
to become too invested in our own lives —
jobs, higher studies or families,

whichever we chose to concentrate in.

*What I had not expected, however,*
*was to be reduced*
*into another name*
*in your contact list.*

# 34. Unconditional



They lie
when they speak of
unconditional love;
such a thing
does not exist
unless
it is between
you
and
the One above.

# 35. Wings Of Flight

There are days
I simply wish
I were a bird.
A bird with no problems,
no worries, no grief, no pain;
no disappointments
or the feeling of being betrayed.

I wish I were a bird;
a bird with nothing to weigh me down,
no chains that drag me to the ground,
no restrictions that render my wings useless.
Whenever I feel like it,
I could spread my wings and fly,
soar high in the sky;
forget about the world for a while.

Sometimes I really wish I were a bird.
Maybe if I were one,
I would not be plagued
by the anguish that usually grips my soul.
Maybe if I were one,
I would not be haunted

by the things that shake me to the core.
Maybe, just maybe,
life could have been better as a bird.

These musings of mine wither away
within moments of their birth.
I mercilessly douse them
with a pint of sanity,
for I'm aware
that if I were a bird
and missed out
on all the hardships I face,
I may never be able to
reap the fruits of my trials,
I may never be able to
meet my Prophet (saw),
never be able to
see His (swt) Face.
I may never be able to
set my eyes on the gardens
He so often speaks about;
the gardens that have been promised
for you and for me.

The world with all its evils
is not exactly what I wish for,
but the thought of the Hereafter

makes it better for me.

# 36. To Be Or Not To Be

• 48 •

I have written all my desires
and whispered all my pleas.
Only my Lord knows what would happen now —
if it would be or would not be.

# 37. Chisels

Certain words —
Are similar to chisels;
Breaking into your skin,
Digging into your flesh,
Tearing your blood vessels,
Twisting,
Turning,
Chipping.
Scraping
And then,
Departing the way they came,
Leaving you
Bleeding,
Writhing
And silently weeping
In pain.

# 38. Two Faces



I wonder
at the words
of people —
something in their hearts,
something else on their lips.

# 39. Flaws

I know all this shall pass
After a while.
I'm very well aware
That all this is a test
But I'm a human being
After all,
With all the flaws
One could possibly possess.
I expect too much from people,
I make the same mistake twice;
I trust too easily
And when it's broken, I fall.
Maybe that's where
My mistake lies —
Instead of trusting only my Lord,
I dare to give it to one and all.

# 40. Full

• 52 •

Fill your heart with love for Allaah,
You'd want for little else.

# 41. Wallflowers

I guess
Some of us
Are just
Good wallflowers
On the making —
Seen, heard
But never felt;
Looked and smiled at,
But never cherished.
Liked, admired even
But never loved.
But this too, I guess
Is a form of blessing in disguise —
Helps us keep our head on our shoulders
And our feet on the ground.

# 42. Peace

Life does get hard on earth,
No one has ever promised
For it to be a breze.
But whenever things get too difficult
To handle,
Look above and remind yourself —
*Verily, with every hardship comes ease.*
*And with every hardship, there is ease.*

# 43. Disguise

Don't mourn
over your hardships,
don't crib
over your misfortune,
don't curse
in pain.
In reality,
they are nothing
but blessings in disguise,
urging you to turn to Allaah
time and again.

# 44. Hidden

If only you could
peep inside of me
and see the scars
that I have neatly stacked
one after another,
each an aftermath
of what
I had to go through,
you wouldn't be asking me
for the things that you do.

*There is only so much
one can endure.*

# 45. End Destination

• 57 •

What is a little pain,
when at the end of it all,
the Lord Himself awaits?

# 46. Puzzle

Each time I think
I've figured you out —
You prove me wrong.

Every time I think
I have grasped
The concept of you —
The intricately designed
Jigsaw puzzle
That you are,
You prove me wrong.

I promise I had thought
I have understood
What you're made of —
Countless of times.

Infinite times had I
Gathered all your pieces
Intending on putting them back
To make you whole.

But each time,

Life happened,
And the breeze blew,
I dropped those puzzle pieces
And I knew
I had lost a piece of you
Forever.

*Life indeed has its own way*
*Of meddling.*
*Each time I settle for something,*
*It proves me wrong.*

# 47. Barricades

If He ever
withheld from you
something
you so badly wanted,
know that,
it was
for your own good.

# 48. Those Days

When the storm clouds hover
And thunder rages ahead,
When walls form closer
And thoughts swirl in my head,
When my heart feels so heavy
And there's nothing I can do,
When the masks start to fall off
And promises prove to be untrue,
When waddling through high tides
And the chasms begin to deepen,
When shards of broken dreams pierce
And awful thoughts start to creep in,
When the words seem to be too many,
And yet, very little make sense,
When the impasse is too steep
And my emotions are intense —
In moments like these,
A desire - so intense assails me
Urging me to go back to those days
When grades were our biggest worries
And snacks - our biggest concern,
When the world seemed pleasant enough
And we had so much to learn,

When tests were what kept us awake
And assignments were what stressed us out,
When parents-teachers meet were our biggest nightmare
And had us unnerved throughout,
When expressions were not pinched
And there were no painted smiles,
When the roads ahead didn't seem endless
Seemingly going on for miles,
When words were not thought over
And laughter was carefree,
When moves were not calculated
And I could just be me.

# 49. Phases

Life indeed
has weird phases,
phases resembling
pieces of jigsaw puzzle
having magnetic property.
Scatter them or shuffle them,
place them around,
or gnore them.
No matter what you do,
you'd find that
at the end of the day,
they have
the knack of coming together
all on their own;
complementing edges
moulding, fitting
with perfection
leaving the beholder
bewitched.

# 50. Words

They come slowly,
little by little
then
all at once —
these words
that act like shrapnel,
piercing,
cutting,
hurting,
and later leaving
a gaping hole behind.

*When will I ever be free of them?*
*Will they even stop being launched at me?*

# 51. Precedence

Fall in love
with Allaah first,
the rest of your world
will fall into place.

# 52. How?

How is that
you don't believe
the One
who created
the entire universe
with all its grandeur
to not make things
perfect
for you?

# 53. Pieces

I am already
A mess of broken pieces,
Don't let me shatter.

# 54. Wait

Just trust Him,
They will eventually go away;
These wounds, those scars, that debilitating pain —
They will eventually go away,
Just trust Him.

# 55. Unanswered Questions

It is one of those days
my thoughts are so muddled,
I cannot even
put them in words
to explain
what is the issue.
My eyes shed silent tears,
my throat thickens
and a sob is contained
with difficulty.

*When will we stop living for the society?*
*When will I stop being seen as a duty?*

# 56. Answerer

• 70 •

He is Al-Mujeeb, The Answerer,
When and what has to be answerered,
He knows it better than you.

# 57. Pills

And
there are some issues
we swallow
like bitter pills,
forcing smiles
on our faces,
pretending
they make us better
when in reality,
they shred us
strand by strand,
dissect us
piece by piece,
unveil us
part by part
and display us
for the ravens to peck.

# 58. Irony

In a way
Isn't love ironic always?

It hurts
When you think it won't,
It takes
When you are expecting it to give;
It shows you valleys
When you are heading to peaks
And stabs
Where you're most susceptible to wounds.

# 59. Sabr

Sabr doesn't mean
Resigning yourself
To your fate;
It means
Having a firm conviction
That Allaah would
Surely find you a way out.
That there would come a day
When you would not
Hurt anymore,
That there would come a day
You wouldn't be tossed aside,
That there would come a day
You wouldn't be
Treated like a nobody,
That there would come a day
You would no longer be tried.
You've just got to believe
That it is only a matter of time.

# 60. Pretense

Tired of pretending
That everything is alright
When I know it's not.

# 61. Hang On

Even if you're being
Peeled on the outside,
Clawed on the inside,
Left feeling hollow,
Re-evaluating your self-worth,
Try sabr — it always pays!
Hold on to that last thread,
Don't give up;
Believe in yourself,
More so in the One who created you!
Even if others leave you hanging,
Remember that He always stays!

# 62. Life

She stared
as they shredded her dreams
into fine threads,
tore her heart
into infinite pieces
she cannot collect,
murdered her feelings
to an extent
that she bled.
She was able to do nothing,
nothing more than stare!

*Life happened after all!*

# 63. Worth The Wait

• 77 •

All this
pain,
heartbreak,
and disappointment
will make sense
one day.

# 64. Time

It works
silently,
wordlessly
but gradually,
breaking the shapeless rock,
chipping off the extra pieces,
working on the form,
on the finer details,
bringing out the finesse,
making it perfect
until
things start taking shape;
until
the best of the best
is born.
If this is common knowledge,
then why moan over the mishaps?
Why stress
over the pain?
Why feel
punctured with helplessness?
Why ever complain?

# 65. Poets

There's nothing fancy
about us poets.
We are just like any of you
in the most mundane way.
Well, except for maybe
in the usage of our words
which is nothing but an attempt
at writing our pain away.

# 66. On Your Screen

I sometimes wonder
about the lost souls,
the forgotten,
the deprived,
the bleeding,
the wounded,
even the unjustly denied.
Is it that the people are blind
or does the media
not focus them
on their screen?

# 67. Warriors Within

I agree that things are so bad love,
so bad that you sometimes
start questioning your existence,
start questining as to why things are
the way they are;
start questioning if we'd ever get to live
without foolish leaders
affecting our lives,
without creeps
plotting against us,
without people spewing Islaamophobic comments
wherever we go,
without receiving nasty glances for veiling ourselves
in a world that appreciates nudity
but guess what love?
The world is not for believers,
never has and will never be.
But that doesn't mean
that we should give up on life or start to lose hope.
It certainly doesn't mean
that we should take to nunnery or turn monks
because that is what our test is all about —
to face challenges, to face difficulties,

to face hate and still live,
still survive by defeating them all.

Remind yourself
that each one of us are warriors within,
inspired by a Prophet (saw)
who stood for what is right
all his life,
and warriors we'd strive to be;
warriors we'd strive to remain.

# 68. Cracks



Few look at me
right in the eye
and smile
in such a sickly, sweet way,
thinking I wouldn't figure it out.
How can I let them know
that I look right through
the cracks in their smiles
and notice all the broken edges?

*If you wouldn't let me,*
*who will mend you?*
*Who will glue back your pieces*
*for you?*

# 69. Stories

Most often than not
the brightest of smiles
conceal
the most painful stories.

# 70. Choices

• 85 •

There is nothing more
soul wrenching,
heart shattering,
mind numbing
than knowing
that you're the second choice
for everyone
in every single thing.

# 71. Rejection

Once a glass falls, cracks
and the shards disperse
in different directions,
you can never put them back,
they will remain what they are —
broken.

So be careful while
dealing with fragile hearts,
they don't take things lightly.
Once you fail their trust,
their affection for you will start to ebb
gradually and steadily.

# 72. No More



I know
that *that* smile
is not directed
towards me anymore.
It's okay,
I will live through.
Just like how
I had been living
even before I met you!

# 73. His Wisdom

Every time
I asked for something
with outstretched palms,
and He denied,
placing something else in them,
I always found
His choice
to be better than mine.


*Indeed He knows best.*

# 74. Murder

How can you even
expect for me
to put it all in the past
and go back
to being normal
after
having sliced me into two?

*Don't you realize*
*it was the murder*
*of not one but two?*

# 75. Untitled

And in moments where
the lack of your existence
weighs me down,
I curl my hand
over where
you once rested
and cry
silent tears
to myself;
in broken words
I whisper to my Lord
and to you,
although I know
you can never hear me.

I'm sorry
for not taking enough
care of you.

I'm sorry
for letting my emotional trauma
reach you.

I'm sorry
for lettting you be added
in biomedical wastes
that would later be incinerated.

I'm sorry
that half the people related to you
did not even deem it decent
to mourn your loss.

I'm sorry
for all that I
put you through.

# 76. Memories

Days rolled into weeks,
weeks into years and yet,
the memories stayed.

# 77. Stain



If only I were to
pour my pain
into the ocean,
you'd be surprised
at how it stains.

# 78. For A Reason

When you have crossed all the deserts,
swam across the shores,
braved all the ditches
and scaled all the mountains,
then, when you look back
on all that you had to endure,
you'd know:
all these hindrances
on the path to eternal gardens —
they were all placed there for a reason.

# 79. From My Heart

A gentle touch,
A cheerful smile,
A soothing speech
Stretching on for miles.

A different persona
With a majestic aura around;
Capable of changing my life
With a sense profound.

Discovering my talents
And igniting my days;
Illuminating my mind
And mending my ways.

A word of encouragement
Making me swell with pride;
Pushing me outside my comfort zone
To a tactful side!

A perfect critic
Warning ahead of time;
Looking into things

And making sure they rhyme.

Each little thing you say,
Every little thing you do
Means a lot to me,
Always has and will ever do.

You're truly way too precocious, ma,
In an impeccable way
And I could never ever deny that
You've made me into who I am today!

# 80. Ethereal Love

I love that I'm able to turn back
After sinning, repenting,
Feeling betrayed by my own,
Feeling rejected
To still find Him there
Waiting for me.

He neither withdraws,
Nor judges,
Wants the best for me
And makes sure I receive it.

I love that I could put my head down
On the ground
And converse with Him,
Feeling His presence embrace me.
I love that I could read His Words,
Drown in them
Only to find calmness surging through me.

He doesn't put me second best,
Instead listens and answers,

Giving me just what I need.

I love how His love exceeds a mother's love,
I love how He provides more than a father,
I love how He helps us more than a friend
And keeps ushering us further.

He knows of all our tears and worries and grief,
Has the answer to all our questions
And the solution to all our affairs.

I love that I'm given freedom,
And rights and choices
Even if others can't get it in their head.
I love how how my faith
Encompasses everything good
And keeps everyone in check.

I love that everything He has forbidden
Has a deeper meaning,
Sometimes so deep
That we cannot even comprehend.

I simply love the fact
That He loves me
And I love that
I'm His slave.